DISCARDED

CALVIN HARRIS
SUPERSTAR DJ

KATIE LAJINESS

Big Buddy Books
An Imprint of Abdo Publishing
abdopublishing.com

BIG BUDDY POP BIOGRAPHIES

abdopublishing.com

Published by Abdo Publishing, a division of ABDO, PO Box 398166, Minneapolis, Minnesota 55439. Copyright © 2018 by Abdo Consulting Group, Inc. International copyrights reserved in all countries. No part of this book may be reproduced in any form without written permission from the publisher. Big Buddy Books™ is a trademark and logo of Abdo Publishing.

Printed in the United States of America, North Mankato, Minnesota.
092017
012018

THIS BOOK CONTAINS RECYCLED MATERIALS

Cover Photo: Jason Merritt/Getty Images
Interior Photos: Adam Bettcher/Getty Images (p. 5); Christopher Polk/Getty Images (pp. 17, 23); Dave J Hogan/Getty Images (p. 19); Ethan Miller/Getty Images (p. 21); Frederick M. Brown/Getty Images (p. 27); Graham Denholm/Getty Images (p. 9); Jim Dyson/Getty Images (p. 13); Kevin Winter/Getty Images (p. 25); Kristian Dowling/Getty Images (p. 11); Pascal Le Segretain/Getty Images (p. 29); Tom Shaw/Getty Images (p. 15).

Coordinating Series Editor: Tamara L. Britton
Contributing Editor: Jill Roesler
Graphic Design: Jenny Christensen

Publisher's Cataloging-in-Publication Data

Names: Lajiness, Katie, author.
Title: Calvin Harris / by Katie Lajiness.
Description: Minneapolis, Minnesota : Abdo Publishing, 2018. | Series: Big buddy pop biographies | Includes online resources and index.
Identifiers: LCCN 2017943936 | ISBN 9781532112157 (lib.bdg.) | ISBN 9781614799221 (ebook)
Subjects: LCSH: Harris, Calvin (Adam Wiles), 1984-.--Juvenile literature. | Disc jockeys--Juvenile literature. | Radio broadcasters--Juvenile literature. | Great Britain--Juvenile literature.
Classification: DDC 781.64092 [B]--dc23
LC record available at https://lccn.loc.gov/2017943936

CONTENTS

MUSIC STAR 4
SNAPSHOT 5
FAMILY TIES 6
EARLY YEARS 8
STARTING OUT 10
RISING STAR 14
MUSICAL LIFE 16
SUPERSTAR DJ 20
SOCIAL MEDIA 22
GIVING BACK 24
AWARDS 26
BUZZ 28
GLOSSARY 30
ONLINE RESOURCES 31
INDEX 32

MUSIC STAR

Calvin Harris is a famous **disc jockey (DJ)**, **producer**, songwriter, and **vocalist**. He is best known for the hits "This Is What You Came For" and "I Need Your Love." Over the years, Calvin has won many **awards** for his music. His songs are popular with fans around the world!

SNAPSHOT

NAME:
Adam Richard Wiles

BIRTHDAY:
January 17, 1984

BIRTHPLACE:
Dumfries, Scotland

POPULAR ALBUMS:
Motion, I Created Disco, 18 Months

FAMILY TIES

Adam Richard Wiles was born in Dumfries, Scotland, on January 17, 1984. His parents are David and Pamela Wiles. He has one sister and one brother, Sophie and Edward.

DID YOU KNOW?
When Adam was growing up, his father was a scientist and his mother was a homemaker.

WHERE IN THE WORLD?

Scotland
NORTH SEA
Dumfries
UNITED KINGDOM
Northern Ireland
ISLE OF MAN
IRELAND
IRISH SEA
Wales
England

EARLY YEARS

As a child, Adam was a shy boy. He liked to spend time alone making music. In 1999, Adam sent **demos** to record companies. Sadly, music **producers** were not interested in his music.

Adam did not give up. In 2002, he **released** a single called "Da Bongos/Brighter Days." At this time, he used the stage name Stouffer.

Life wasn't always fun for Adam. At 16, he became ill and missed a year of school.

STARTING OUT

Adam's single did not lead to instant success. After high school, he continued to live with his parents. In his free time, Adam worked on his music.

In 2003, Adam moved to London, England, for a year. There, he **released** "Let Me Know" with singer Ayah. During this time, he changed his stage name to Calvin Harris.

For a while, Calvin worked in a bakery. He spent his money on new music equipment.

Even with a new stage name and music, Calvin still had a hard time. He wanted people to listen to his work.

When he was 21, Calvin posted his songs on **social media**. A **producer** loved "Acceptable in the 80s" and "The Girls." Soon, a record company wanted Calvin to write music for other artists.

In 2006, Calvin signed a deal with EMI Records. A year later, he wrote and produced songs for singer Kylie Minogue.

Calvin wrote and produced "In My Arms" for Australian singer Kylie Minogue.

RISING STAR

After years of struggle, Calvin had become a rising star. Soon, he signed with Columbia Records to **release** his own music.

In 2007, Calvin released *I Created Disco*. It became a top 20 album on the *Billboard* Top Electronic Albums chart.

"Acceptable in the 80s" and "The Girls" became hit songs for Calvin.

MUSICAL LIFE

Finally, Calvin was a famous music **producer** and writer. In 2009, he **released** the album *Ready for the Weekend*. Calvin spent much of the next year on a world tour.

In 2011, he and **pop** star Rihanna released "We Found Love." The song earned worldwide success and topped the *Billboard* chart for eight weeks.

Calvin performed at the 2012 iHeartRadio Music Festival in Las Vegas, Nevada.

Soon, many singers wanted to work with Calvin. In 2012, he **released** his third major album, *18 Months*. It featured the song "I Need Your Love" with British singer Ellie Goulding. The single sold 1 million copies in the United States!

Calvin continued to write songs. Two years later, he put out another album, *Motion*. It sold well, but the album was not as successful as his others.

More than 50,000 fans enjoyed Calvin's performance at BBC Radio 1's 2014 Big Weekend in Glasgow, Scotland.

SUPERSTAR DJ

Calvin's dance music was so popular, people wanted to hear him live. So, he became a **DJ** at dance clubs in Las Vegas, Nevada.

He became known for his **unique** sound. Fans loved listening to Calvin's music outside of the club. "This Is What You Came For" sold 2 million copies. And "How Deep Is Your Love" sold more than 1 million copies.

DID YOU KNOW?
Calvin earned $66 million in 2014. This made him the world's highest-paid DJ.

In 2013, Calvin became the long-term headliner at the MGM Grand's Hakkasan Las Vegas nightclub.

SOCIAL MEDIA

Calvin has been quite popular on **social media**. In 2017, he had nearly 10 million followers on Twitter. And, more than 8 million people followed him on Instagram.

Fans couldn't get enough of his music. "This Is What You Came For" was viewed more than 1 billion times on the website YouTube!

Fans took note when Calvin deleted and then added singer Taylor Swift on social media.

GIVING BACK

Calvin has taken time to give back to those in need. In 2007, he **performed** at an event for a **charity** called CALM. This group helps people who are very sad.

He was also a **DJ** at the Wickerman Festival. There, Calvin helped raise money for a housing charity called Shelter Scotland.

Calvin was a DJ at the 2015 We Can Survive benefit. This group supports young women with an illness called cancer.

AWARDS

DID YOU KNOW?
Calvin won Solo Artist of the Year at the 2016 GQ Men of the Year Awards.

Calvin is an **award**-winning artist. In 2012, he and Rihanna won a **Grammy Award** for "We Found Love." They took home the Best Short Form Music Video award.

The next year, Calvin received the 2013 Ivor Novello Award for Songwriter of the Year. He called it "the greatest **achievement** of my life."

Calvin has also won several MTV Music Awards.

BUZZ

Over the years, this talented **DJ** has created fun dance music. Throughout 2017, Calvin continued to **perform** in Las Vegas. He also **released** more hit music. Fans are excited to see what Calvin does next!

DID YOU KNOW?
Calvin's summer hit "Heatstroke" featured rapper Young Thug, Pharrell Williams, and singer Ariana Grande.

Calvin's single "Slide" featured Frank Ocean and Migos. The song reached number 34 on the Hot 100 chart.

GLOSSARY

achievement a result gained by effort.

award something that is given in recognition of good work or a good act.

charity a group or a fund that helps people in need.

demo a recording to show a musical group or artist's abilities.

disc jockey (DJ) one who plays recorded music for dancing at a nightclub or party.

Grammy Award any of the awards given each year by the National Academy of Recording Arts and Sciences. Grammy Awards honor the year's best accomplishments in music.

perform to do something in front of an audience.

pop relating to popular music.

produce to oversee the making of a movie, a play, an album, or a radio or television show. A producer is a person who oversees the making of a movie, a play, an album, or a radio or television show.

release to make available to the public.

social media a form of communication on the Internet where people can share information, messages, and videos. It may include blogs and online groups.

unique (yu-NEEK) being the only one of its kind.

vocalist singer.

To learn more about Calvin Harris, visit **abdobooklinks.com**. These links are routinely monitored and updated to provide the most current information available.

INDEX

awards **4, 26, 27**

Ayah **10**

BBC Radio 1 **19**

charities **24, 25**

Columbia Records **14**

18 Months (album) **5, 18**

EMI Records **12**

England **10**

family **6, 10**

Goulding, Ellie **18**

Grande, Ariana **28**

Hakkasan **21**

I Created Disco (album) **5, 14**

iHeartRadio Music Festival **17**

MGM Grand **21**

Migos **29**

Minogue, Kylie **12, 13**

Motion (album) **5, 18**

music charts **14, 16, 29**

Nevada **17, 20, 21, 28**

Ocean, Frank **29**

Ready for the Weekend (album) **16**

Rihanna **16, 26**

Scotland **5, 6, 19**

social media **12, 22, 23**

Stouffer **8**

Swift, Taylor **23**

United States **18**

Wickerman Festival **24**

Williams, Pharrell **28**

Young Thug **28**